MW01278242

The LAST HOUSE

Also by Michael Kenyon

Fiction

Kleinberg (Oolichan Books)
Pinocchio's Wife (Oberon)
Durable Tumblers (Oolichan Books)
The Biggest Animals (Thistledown Press)
The Beautiful Children (Thistledown Press)

Poetry

Rack of Lamb (Brick Books)
The Sutler (Brick Books)

The LAST HOUSE

MICHAEL KENYON

Brick Books

Library and Archives Canada Cataloguing in Publication

Kenyon, Michael, 1953-
    The last house / Michael Kenyon.

Poems.
ISBN 978-1-894078-74-0

    I. Title.

PS8571.E67L37 2009   C811'.54   C2009-902316-4

We acknowledge the Canada Council for the Arts, the
Government of Canada through the Book Publishing Industry
Development Program (BPIDP), and the Ontario Arts Council
for their support of our publishing program.

The cover painting is a detail from "Stream" by Lorraine
Thomson. Acrylic and mixed media, 2003.

The author photograph was taken by Lorraine Thomson.

The book is set in Frutiger and Sabon.

Design and layout by Alan Siu.

Printed and bound by Sunville Printco Inc.

Brick Books
431 Boler Road, Box 20081
London, Ontario N6K 4G6

www.brickbooks.ca

For Lorraine and Ashlan

Contents

Broke   13   I
Splinter   15
Feast   17
Exposure   19

Trace   23   II
Light Blinds the Helm   30
This Is True   33

Lost Countryside   III

Chimney   41
Manchester   42
Cheshire   43
When Hawks Stop Hunting   44
Vernacular   45
Lost Countryside   46
Dumpster   47
Subdivision   48
Direct Totem   49
Broken Roof   50

Tenement

Mobile Home   51
Cellar   52
Tenement   53
Basement Suite   54
Hotel Garden   55
James Bond Above the Palace Gate   56
Townhouse   57
The Ruined Cottage   58

Quit This Ground   61

Picker's Sons   63

Hand   67

The Last House   69

Papa Chaos   75

Wren   82

IV

Courtyard

V

Middle Region   85

Courtyard   86

Leap   87

This Perfect   88

Hit Brightness with Brightness   89

Georgia Strait   90

Sorcerer   91

The Axe of Change   92

Ancestors   93

Invention of Flight   94

The Stars   95

Utter   96

Chorale   101

Géza   106

VI

Acknowledgements   109

Biography   111

Who has twisted us around like this, so that no matter what we do, we are in the posture of someone going away?

– Rainer Maria Rilke

I

Broke

Once I built a tower, up to the sun,
brick, and rivet, and lime.
Once I built a tower, now it's done.
Brother, can you spare a dime?
                    – Yip Harburg

Dad planned the old stone pile from the top
down with a fine view of rolling hills
and woods in the distance, the village
spire fixed in clouds, and provided me
every day of phlogistic childhood
with nothing but the hedge path to run
fast to school and slow home each winter
night. Weekends were blue tropical fish
by steam train for my aquarium.
Once I built a tower to the sun

that lit England the same way the bulb
lit the fish. After school kids tunnelled
under Bluebell Woods till October
submerged the cricket field in fog and
houses sprang up like mushrooms over
the hills. School and home and work and home
all mesh, as do fish, tunnel, train, each
stolen plank and nail, candle for our
cave, even flattened earth and green slime,
brick, and rivet, and lime.

Granddad did time by the fire. Fixed
clocks with glue. Corine Davis' knickers
caught a nail, and I saw a man in
shirtsleeves dance on the windy street and
promised myself to burn like him, burn,
buddy-boy, attenuate, starve. Come,
full-blood guttersnipe, desert foal, this
day between school and home will flip and
all will pass, and all you set out from.
Once I built a tower, now it's done.

Now sparks coruscate this half-new world,
its low roofs like bottle caps under
which we huddle, bright drunk folk, to work
small and gigantic – fieldstone, hill end,
clear-cut, pasture, dairy, army – lies,
enough to pay the bills and not mind
how much we owe the black earth and sky,
east and west. How we night-sail, sail top-
heavy, waiting for the nick of time.
Brother, can you spare a dime?

Splinter

You were inside my hand.
I kept reaching around for something.
I was inside your hand, but I kept asking questions
Of those who knew very little.

  – Rumi

I was small and well away from the world
when mistletoe on the left of the path
fell from its host so the gate lay open.
The ocean between what I had left and
what I had rippled with significance
and all night I flew above the dark planed
surface till I got to the mainland coast,
blacktop, mall, the line of shops where shoppers
blindly shopped, and stepped through the broken land.
You were inside my hand,

tame as a heart I didn't want,
and small and well away from the
world, a knot, nest, fraction, puzzle,
quite safe, I thought, from human loss
and struggle, and safe enough from
harm because poor enough to bring
neither envy nor attention.
You were sweet with time, complex as
a hooded hawk. You were one thing
I kept reaching around for, something

to hang onto, something to buy, a box
of shells or jar of jam. I was going
to make up my own world on the left of
the path behind the mall in the small woods
where the living tree had split from lightning
and split the rock it grew on. The best guns
were my best friends who all had new rifles
and shot at birds in the dead branches. Our
fort collapsed. Our school burned. We were best sons.
I was inside your hand, but I kept asking questions

of the spark inside my hand; now
both of us are hooded. Friends fade.
Business fails. Only wind stirs the
ocean between what we have and
what we have lost. Only hunger
stirs the pot. Flag ropes tap brittle
poles, and the open-mouthed crowd turns
into motes. Your wings opened and
I flew above the dark metal
of those who knew very little.

Feast

> Now come, the last that I can recognize,
> pain, utter pain, fierce in the body's texture.
> As once in the mind I burned, so now I burn
> in you; the wood resisted, long denied...
>
>   – Rilke

A child in winter under the sickle
moon one moment is bright with play, in love
with candy, lips and fingers Smartie red
(she likes red best), cartwheels on black branches,
oak branches written by wind and street lamp
on the hardwood floor, next moment's surprised
by a cloud that mixes moon with sweetness,
cartwheel with voices from the kitchen, Mum
and Auntie, who discuss olives and lies.
Now come, the last that I can recognize,

old mountain beacon that holds fast sun's light,
tell us a story, tell us a tale, bring
news of wealth, gold, the latest adventures
of heros adrift far from shore, no wind,
oarless, trying to get home by dreams of
red cows full of milk in such green pasture
focaccia, arugula, lettuce,
balsamic vinegar and oil, white plates,
rectory table, subtract from pleasure
pain, utter pain, fierce in the body's texture.

That moon, that child, divide heaven's promise
between them; the good food turns grey when day's
hue is absorbed, and streets, hedges, palings,
all turn grey. Then mortal families gather,
women's lies no stronger than lies of men,
too flushed to sit down, while the children learn
there's slippage, a hole in the sky, the skin,
some wrong thing among us that burns and burns
the way wine, dark red, dries the throat and burns.
As once in the mind I burned, so now I burn

to heal this hurt child, light new white candles,
start the feast. She tells us she's dizzy, can't
stand the noise. All lies cease, laughter bows out.
When a child sickens in January, spring
breaches. A branch taps the window. She runs
in circles. With no one sober we hide
our fear and call a cab. Again the rush
of sudden fog: I'm in my first forest,
mouth zeroed. O trees, I want to confide
in you; the wood resisted, long denied...

Exposure

> He posed us near our tent's propped flap,
> my parents shy against its wing, my toddler sister
> tucked below, then waved us to a sudden freeze –
>
> – Linda Bierds

Fifty-three years of struggle since
our family blew west and off
the sea to the dust of this hill.
One day my uncle took me down-
river to the big cave to shoot
morning swallows and listen hard
for frog, bird, water, cloud. Human
footprints, a large set and a small,
led beneath the cliff to a boat
painted red. He rowed out of green
currents into the foaming black
waves. We sat face to face all day,
and when we returned to the cave
he posed us near our tent's propped flap.

The foot, first with claws, then roots. A herd
of planted feet, too many to count,
so far and small that the pattern flies
at me like my mother's blue dress when
I was young, a flock of birds, seabirds,
sweeping the sky, the blue cave walls chock
full of feet marching to where the stone
ceiling crushes the cold red clay floor.
Before others arrive my uncle
gives me crayons, and I draw a gold
creature with vast wings and a splinter
of light between its eyes. To hold time
still he plants a tripod in the sand.
My parents shy against its wing, my toddler sister

snug between its thighs. Years later
Dad's grin is strained and Mum's eyes glass –
their lives tangled in the frame. Caught.
In me they see faint reflection,
Dad of his own childhood, and Mum
of what's to come. The heat of one,
the chill of the other. Mother's
dress against her body. Dad's glance
at the red boat outside the cave.
My sister's mouth wide. At my desk
I watch night wind blow smoke through trees.
The frame arbitrary, rough edge
snagging threads that Uncle quickly
tucked below, then waved us to a sudden freeze –

II

Trace

The Mall

In the fierce barbaric stage of our dis-
integration Trace turns slim-blonde and ends
the rich age of ram's horn curls with gold lights
and from behind is a different woman,
no longer mine. In tight jeans her ass cheeks
crowd every quick step away while I rub
my hands together like Grandfather did
when he'd forgotten who we were, his hands
squeezing his fingers, then hiding themselves
like small feral creatures, half-asked questions,
beneath the sheets before we had a chance

to respond. I observe her waist, thickened
slightly by years, suddenly narrow and
her neck go slender, hostile. Her hair is
a snow curtain, her shoulder blades ice picks
under the T-shirt. Tough nipples stencil
a crease in the sky-blue cotton. Something
is up in her life. Every single man
stares as she shops. Every man's gaze shocked
at how clear the lips of her cunt are through
the old denim, the fabric so threadbare
both thighs hint at pale skin, the edges of

what I'm allowed to recall, that my great-
great-great-great-grandfather, cockstunned, strained to
see his niece's arse as she bent over
the second floor railing. Knickers made him
lose where and who he was, negotiate
where and who he might be, sharp ferocious
nib part way down the page, all the way down,

loosing an avalanche, till I stand gob-
smacked at Tracy's feet watching a stream surge
along a tiled trough. When she stops to check
herself at the window of a sporting

goods store, boys gather round the reflection
with a magnifying glass to study
the path light takes through cloth and how it treats
the weave and skin, each bump a planet, each
strand a rupture in time, each blue sheath, brown
indent. Before shopping, such cathedrals
inspired Great-Great-Great-Great-Great-Grandfather,
hurt boy and murderer with most crimes un-
seen, to drop many in the village pond
to be nibbled by snakes and frogs whose stirred
world transformed to welcome each stage of life,

species, generation. Meanwhile, she's smug.
She knows she looks good. Grins at her image
in the window, soft lips parted for when
she'll drop to her knees, invite the boys to
rivers that overflow old boundary stones
she's swallowed and swallowed, till they are in
ruins. We all want surprise. A quick chill.
A giggle. But not tears, not this crying.
I'm wet as a fish clothed in air, strangely
well and unafraid. Her safety is up
to mall security cops who step in,

three furies, Defeat, Revenge, Victory.
I know this official version and know
the sequence by heart and wash my hands of
the slow drama, my greyest ancestor,
the guards who lead her to the nearest wall.

She says to stop and wind sighs through the mall.
First guard arrests the boys. Second guard leans
into her. The third uncaps his ballpoint.
And again the years fill with sperm and spleen.
The first stage our eyes. The second our ears.
Third our heart. How easy she is to peel!

I push through the crowd and the guards and get
ready to tell the truth for once and hold
forth loud, for now she's a girl I once loved,
too young to know what's real, just like me, both
of us too young to squeeze meaning out of
our years, much less out of parents long dead.
Ghosts collapse like plastic bags while uncles
in uniform take the glossy floor and
shoppers' voices almost drown the slap of
oars, the flop of landed trout. Death's close. Lungs
fill with earth, my own breath close to drowning.

Glass

Outside the neighbour's greenhouse brews a storm
lopsided with rain. I tell him about
Tracy and watch him pick a cucumber
and toss it in a swampy raised bed where
there's thrashing and a plosive gasp, supple
slide of a long thick black body; he laughs.
"The eel is hungry." Then silence, complete.
Humid. Intimate. We're not who we were.
It's evening, when malevolence lingers
in every bulbous and rotting green thing
and marsh lights flicker out across the fields.

I wade home through the stubble, press my face
to the ground-floor window to see a man
inside Tracy, the bed an unmade nest,
the air violet with flying splinters.
A sudden inhalation from the crowd.
Their bodies can't figure what to protect,
who is dream, who is real, what here, what there.
As I climb through the bloody broken glass,
Uncles grab Tracy's arms so I can tilt
my cock to her open mouth. Amazement.
We are all harmed by what we have made clear.

Overall

And so her face grows shy, her eyes drop mine.
Nipples finger the coarse denim. A white
half moon shines each side of the blue tunic.
She says, "Look at it this way." Visible
waist a milk-curve down into the garment's
dark scoop and deeper, sharp hips and deeper:
tide line on a still sea, a clean red row
of tiny rose buds, the tattoo artist
crouched intent over low-slung beads of blood.
Her belly. Her breath a rise and fall. "You
wouldn't want me if you hadn't lost me."

When we met in philosophy she said
Ludwig Wittgenstein was sexy. I said
Herakleitos of Ephesos said war
was the father of all things. She said leave
that be. We hit my place because she was
living in her Volvo. Her dentist was,

she said, the image of Ludwig. I said
Herakleitos lived in the same city
all his life. Ephesos, she said, and whipped
out a brand new toothbrush. Bless you, I said.
After olives and beer we fucked six times.

The curtain rises and the room's full of
long shadows rippling as she floats across
roofs and through windows to rooms where couples
lit by television come apart or
together and mean something. Her back wears
a cross: this is yours always: these wrists in
the circle of your fingers against wood –
trees or walls. This blood is yours and the quiet
of the city. A country's thousand long
nights. Cock's crow outside the house of ribbons
returned to after an absence of life.

Home

Again I knock at the door, lose myself
a moment in the storm. The house seems still,
a sombre pile of hollow rooms, while wind
behind me hurls debris against cars and
trees and amplifies the clatter and roar
of the mall. I knock again, everything
in turmoil – sticks, leaves, bags, cans, foil wrappers,
branches groaning huge in the tumbling dusk.
All Grandfather's best friends died under fire
in the war. Long lines of cars undulate
as they skewer the mall. This is the gate

between two worlds. Icy fingers catch at
the roots of my hair. Then the door opens
with a click and I'm a child diminished
in the muted light that bathes and haloes
the calm silhouette in the hallway. "Yes?"
She will not recognize me so I kick
shut the door, pin her arms to the wall. "Stay."
This is the atomic state of affairs.
Wittgenstein of the trenches come. Kneel at
her feet to pick each thread of each seam with
the sharp knife from the telephone table.

The cat pads through the hallway, purrs against
my thigh and Tracy does not stare at me,
transfixed, but looks down pityingly while
winter blows against the house and her legs
bloom goosebumps. I don't know what to do so
rattle the door in its hinges and track
the fat snow along the concession road
to the men in town to exchange rounds of
whisky chased with beer, check out the barmaid,
fuck this and fuck that, cat got your tongue? If
you want pussy here's what. Tracy always

wears overalls and nothing else when she's
aiming to get laid, and if her hair's in
a pony tail she's into something quick
as frost, I mean, you can open her like
a ripe tomato, a fresh fig, a grape,
the way the dentist did her mouth to check
her bite, see what makes the enterprise tick,
belly, tits and. Lord save us. This forest
protect us, amen. Let rain follow sun.
Only words. Wittgenstein, Herakleitos,
come to the disco, come. She will dance like

a cat on hot coals. We will be uncles
who want more than skin, more than blood, who want
each rib snapped free, the cage open to see
what flies out and what's sucked in, unlawful
lungs and heart, our own dark secrets. We'll bare
muscle, sinew, our dry girl on the street
to flirt and flick her skirt, show her pelvis
and spine. But she's gone. Puff! Gone for a smoke
between dances. Mountains hidden by night,
night by cloud. Adult by child. Villagers
shiver as they pass her by. Each time less,

she's dressed in rags at the bottom of war.
Herakleitos of Ephesos come. Come.
Forget her hair, forget her face, forget
her tits and her waist. Every girl is young.
Uncles are famous and want her taken
until days flicker twenty-four flames
a second and wankers arrest themselves
in the act and hike down from the mountains.
Trees of this river valley protect us.
Remember the gentle spring, the hawthorn
leafing. The chorus of frogs in the pond.

Light Blinds the Helm

For the cast & crew of *The Winter's Tale*, Vancouver 2006

History

Hurricane. Yellow islands. These are true.
Slaves escape into equatorial
waters, are swallowed. The Master survives
a mutiny off the Blue Coast, the ship
becalmed for twenty-three days, hurricane,
yellow hills. These are true. Slaves dive into
southern waters. The sailors mutiny.
The ship is becalmed for twenty-three days.
Very true, the Captain's story, not tame
before it's written. Bare hills. Hurricane.
Twice I exit the ship, enter the waves.

My father wants light in the world, a path
sparking water to nearest land, same light
that blinds the helm this third voyage into
open ocean. I have never been here
before. All is new except the water,
except the light. What shows the way confounds
the senses. When we turn to instruments,
we refuse nature, we doubt our bodies.
My father wants light. My father wants light.
I can't let what happened happen again.
Light is nothing but what it hits upon.

I cast about, still blinded by the sun
that set an hour ago, for the North Star,
and hot vivid winds blow up from the south,
the churning deck too quick for my square bones,
yet slow for the new dog at heel, engrossed
with my foot, her big paws gaining purchase
where there's none. She looks through me. I can't see

the end of her, nor profit in being
lost again, the ship framed by hurricane
that seems to speak of home and sleep, silk slide
of sky across the mate's worried stubble.

Nature's ruin refuses our eyes. Once.
Uniforms swaying on hangers and words
floating backward, whence, whence? Notice I give
the world notice instead of noting salt
on my skin? Yet on this ocean no war
rises or sets. Clouds drift, wrack above wrack.
Nature's ruin refuses our eyes. Twice.
At home the principals await jewels,
and zoological societies
expect specimens to prove their theories.
The rock headlands refuse my hands three times.

Rescue

Actors – stage a deck, custom overturned –
are sailors, seabirds scratching the tide wrack
for dropped lines and cues and hurricane lamps
while carpenters unfurl the torn rigging.
This dream. That audience. Even the play.
All made out of scraps of old scaffolding
from earlier storms. This rowboat intact.
Miraculous oars raised high like palm fronds,
their varnish a mirror in which I see
eight versions of my old weak face tricky
as a coconut almost howling glee.

Comedy No

We're rehearsing a tragedy, later
days, centuries on, director calling
for consciousness of ideas, more *nose*
and *eyebrows*, and less wind in the tent, for
the performance will be in a small cove
on the coast, above the rocks, even though
it is late in the year. They expect me
to take the role of son and king. Funding
is mine because they have borrowed against
my return. The celebration hopeful,
tragedy incomplete, my friends all here.

'Play, boy, play'

And the word is carved inside a cartoon
heart on the 1926 sidewalk
the southwest corner of Third and Blenheim
and I go there most nights before falling
asleep to bring the *Tale*, my family,
from time into Time. We have never seen
such light in the world. Such light in the world.
Autolycus rubs hands and face in dirt.
The shepherd and the shepherd's son run lines
outside the green room. And Mamillius,
my boy, rides his bike through the summer night.

This Is True

Dog

You are wrapped in a green blanket the soil
presses down, paws folded so, nails too long,
whiskers as puzzled as ever. Trees rise
from broken rock in green old age, the themes
now obvious to all, even to me,
my arms locked around my body, its bones,
to keep breath at bay, the blanket's smell gone
with the rest of you. The cold weather breaks
and instead of snow it rains hard, and rain
pools the ground where you get set for spring and
for us to hike over the hills again.

After the Wreck

Granddad comes in a dream to tell me, "What
you work on works on you." When I ask him
how he is, he says fine thanks, pretty good,
he has been pressing black olives in Greece.
You swam by my side into the shell beach,
then shook, wagged your tail, and put your nose down.
The swell-fed sailors roll ashore next day,
pragmatic, assuring me with their eyes
that I'm no use here. Past the farthest rock
the tide runs fast and surf leaps in the air.
Out there we flailed in a monstrous current.

Unlost dog. Black-eyed Susan. Running stream.
What are we? Brown hills. Dislocated palms.
Still cogent in a land where nothing is
familiar. I'm the body of sadness,

homesick, while you find the path and lead me
through the bush, torn between signals, your nose
a mouse across just-cooled magma, that old
evolution chestnut and the sweet heart
song: lost and going where your master goes,
as old as the moon in thrall to this world.
And for a moment I can see us both

as bureaucrats and connoisseurs of sin
on the hunt for gold and a piece of tail,
all clues gone. We don't belong here. Not lost,
just jittery and unoriented.
A cigarette would do the trick. I dreamed
of a standing ewe with lamb in a field
in America. A thin woman past
forty against the black-and-white skyline.
Gaunt pieces. I don't recognize myself.
On the white-shell beach crows huddle to pull
bones over the dead regardless of tide.

What We Have

Not much longer now. A joke. Small waves, hills,
horizon, hills, horizon, all gathered
for the straggler, the newcomer. Heron
boredom, glitter fish, inadequacy.
With whole shells from the beach I try to mark
my place. When I was young I'd walk into
a forest and be in a magical
work, separated from the common parts
of life by new paths that led to clearings
thick with incense, with walls of climbing vines.
Years later the story continues. Time

doffs its wings, abandons its abacus.
Exile breathes in the fat shadows of trees.
I give up listing my different selves,
measuring the distance from outside to
inside, from urban to rural. The thump
of a grouse intersects the jet's thin jazz.
The walls of this world are quite soft and rain
on palm fronds whispers like people coming
through the forest whose floor unleashes green
heads of new ferns. I keep going over
the same ground. Ghosts, music, all under wraps.

Where's the ribbon to prettify things now
there's nowhere that is not connected to
everywhere else? Grass will cover the tracks
of whatever has passed. There is no end
to the love of animals. Story's not
empty either. Wild mint, sage, licorice.
At home cilantro escaped into lawn
so next year's mowing smashed the air with spice.
The warmth of stepping into your brown gaze.
In the middle of the bird call is this
difficult task of husbandry. Inside

the forest is a tower of bones, moss-
green, and an alley wide as a desert.
We call this emptiness, at least I do,
not knowing what else to hold, having lost
the need to nurture and all of the names
but yours, dog. And after you go I'll have
these non-sequiturs visit like demons
each time I set out from the shell beach, you
at heel, in memory or metaphor
no matter, to wind up at this clearing,
this heap of bones resembling less and less

the building I once fooled myself into
believing I'd made, mnemonic tower,
my beginning and end, my dead fellow
sailors. Green! All season the ferns shout green!
In the bone room bats fly. I remember
finding something hidden in a drawer.
Hard among soft or soft in hard. Secret.
You killed a duck. Yes, true, you killed a duck.
She was dying anyway, disembowelled
by an eagle. You brought her to me, so
warm in my arms, a bundle of feathers.

I feel the weight lift sometimes as we walk.
All is not quite lost or not quite all lost.
A specific here. Lifting joy when you
run and something in me links to something
in you. But always when we are alone.
Alone is the trick. Alone is the trick.
What particulars about the universe
are we hungry for? You're the only way
to my forgotten self, my human self.
I dreamed I found you in a Banyan tree.
Love me? *I would, Master, were I human.*

Meanwhile

Back home my parents wait on the hillside
for a sign. Meanwhile the creditors play
poker. Meanwhile I grow older and cry
hard at night because a dog will not live
as long as a man. You sleep hard against
my body, state fluid, metamorphic,
neither here nor there nor illusory,

and wake to regard me as though the world
assembles itself just for us and we
are its gods. Gentle mist on the water,
no other land beyond. The tide creeps in.

In my mouth a bitter taste. Fingers quit
fretting eyebrows, mouth, cheek; instead demand
ribs, scapulae, skull. For three days crows and
pigeons, disturbed not at all by you, dog,
have sat their nests. Meanwhile a man murders
his wife, their young, himself. Meanwhile fortunes
raise palaces and temples and vandals
tear them down. We know what we are doing.
But here, among ragged trees and smoking
sun, I find a stone with a white circle
as drops of rain fall from the sky's belly.

Today I am angry. You know to keep
away and sulk at the treeline or limp
ahead on the path. You are a faker.
What happens next has to be made out of
the rhythm of life. Not the life we've left,
but this experiment in paradise,
this repository of deficits.
You're not listening. Whatever moves is
alive, destined for wisdom. What is still,
say death, will be optioned purely as flesh,
immutable, decay offset by this

saturated fantasy. The dog who
drowned, this one alive. Not letting go is
the same as never starting anything
new. This is new. This is. And this. And this.
I never look at you the way you look
at me. I can never see our palm hut

beside the beach by the groaning ocean
without being on the ocean. The sea
ahead is empty; the dark land behind,
after an hour's wait, fills with loud birds.
The hardest thing to bear is night and cold.

After Rescue

And after your own journeys you come to
my side when I call and curl at night by
my bed on the street in the doorway, rain
a river down the sidewalk, passersby
another weather harder to fathom
than solitude or family. That's it
then. Morning grey in the sky. That's it then.
No more voyages. Another beggar
among beggars all done with stories. No
need to prove faithfulness, what life itself
never could prove, no need to look further

than the tiny waves of illness rolling
from the horizon, blue and silver, that
will slowly drown us. And we will go down
easy, man and dog, red and pale, go down
into the green following dark, chased light,
down derry down by all that has and has
not served, in spite of doom, in spite of lives,
and together most important, fishes
quick from our starry shadows blooming
last pale and last red, last lazy spin slow
together and dim, each I remember.

Lost Countryside

Chimney

Here is a nice house with the right number
of bricks and fourteen windows, seven up,
seven down, one door in and one door out
and a chimney top left as you face front.
The west wall is plumb, sheer, perfectly smooth,
the east a jagged series of platforms.
A man in the upper storey gazes
north from the topmost window at nothing.
He's interested only in himself.
The stairs are dark, thick with ghosts. Old questions
hang in the air with dust from the woodstove.
The south-facing rooms shimmer with angled
light that liquifies time and space. His wife
sweeps through a sun lozenge to the kitchen.

Manchester

Mothers weave Lancashire cloth, fathers dig
the Ship Canal to mix rivers with sea,
and I slip away down and past the locks,
hands in pockets, from that epitome,
caricature of human endeavor,
institution, before I get a chance
to read the writing on the wall or jot
a word or two about the sacrifice.
I sail away and buy a house and fall
in love. In a new country you neither
belong nor don't but hope to guess your soul's
purpose. Maybe a bright stillness, a kind
water, a safe cave for your flesh and blood,
a future with history as a slub.

Cheshire

Fresh tulips grey with dust on a flat rock,
sea and sky west, a faint track east all green
across the continent to the sunrise
we sailed past, and Liberty into New York,
a sea path to our teapot home where hours
old I clung to black fury, dark bruises
from the forceps that hauled me out, Mum on
tiptoe on the hospital bed, twenty-
six and shocked by the garden's black tulips,
first she'd seen, an after-shock of Granddad
in France, a rumble deeper than normal
trench terror, and here they come together,
fairy-tale siblings headed home from war
along the faint road west to this hillside:
Granddad's black tanks, mother's coal-black tulips,
and my own black fury, the first ever.

When Hawks Stop Hunting

When hawks stop hunting the farmland I make
a cage of my forearms and trap my chest,
then chest and neck, then chest and neck and skull.
How pointless to hunt when expectation
of disappointment dominates the kill.
I will steal a cabbage and snap flowers
from the bloody hedge, and on my way home
will practice what I know – cultivation
of disappointment – and tonight in bed
will perfect the cage and trap my life and
death so none of my soul will leach away
(the problem is how to spend time and flesh
until nothing stands between bones and sky),
and all I ask is you avert your eye.

Vernacular

Not a big story, a little one, of
down into dark, only wind and sun off-
stage to provoke the heart-shaped flicker
across a line not to be crossed, quicker
along the watery path and then deep,
fast beneath the tremor of yellow leaves,
end of an era, start of a new phase –
no story at all but a new species
of quiet. And so the hills of Dad's bed
in September sunshine. Sea at the end
of the road. Curtains quietly open
to cottonwoods against the slow green slope.
No matter. A perfect, perfect blue day.
He took forever to leave me this tale.

Lost Countryside

A springtime of rain and not much sun, one
death amid thoughts of death, grief a constant
ache in the throat, the word *sing*, prefix of
single, and the walnut in the cracked shell.
I pry it open with a knife. Hemi-
spheres. Two halves of something adored for its
wholeness. Hawk overhead quite curious.
I taste the crumbs of white flesh, familiar,
yes, I've been here before. The black walnut
and guardian woodpecker watched me crouch
to collect nuts while guiding the mower
with one hand. I filled my pockets each fall.
A cloud climbs the sky and someone down
the valley blows a muffler. You know, a thing
of importance will never end, never
be final. I forgot the nuts till one
rolled out of my summer trousers, hung on
the line at the start of spring.

Dumpster

This latest device is for the thin man
without a home, a surefire public boon
I dare say, but not mine, not yet. I read
obituaries as my own although
a raindrop into sea is more my style
as I hike the hills of the old man's farm,
original fields once woods now slated
for new housing me and sis will turn to
profit. Signs nod in September sunshine.
Unheard sea at the end of the blacktop.
But the road is no matter. Mum and Dad
taught us to deflect blame and to save face
and to stay away from fortune and fame.
They took forever and left us this place.

Subdivision

I'm pinned to the back wall of the room by
the blast and when the smoke clears there's a track
out of all we've built. The swamp is foul to
wade through. Where is the sweet meadow? How do
we get there? What force but that which flung us
here will know we sang a garden, *sanctus*,
a grapevine at the pivot point. Atom-
smashers, we hunted the crack in the use
of it all and forgot the bloody news
till air exploded. Pissed, we yodelled heart-
break raw enough to snag the universe.
Wake up, dizzybones, keep your pecker up –
it's too late maybe but you catch the drift.
Step by stagger by step will find the path.

Direct Totem

I'm sorry for the fort we made of steel
because it will reach and cut children who
run through years from now when trunks have rotted,
butterflies gone west, sunlight got lost, and
grey cinders have replaced leaves, nothing in
the rock, nothing in the ruins, no one
to remember how inside metal walls
we slept, the girl by herself and the man
by himself, kept from falling by beak and
talons, our backs to the south wall, heads turned
right for the sunrise, then backs to the north,
faces flamed with sunset, night terrors crouched
amid the shadows of oaks and tigers,
loosestrife, instinct, quartz hunter, firelight.

Broken Roof

In the spring when hedges have leaves again
I'll watch for my mum in the wild places
and look for Dad in faces of strangers,
every village and town, this winter far
too cold to try much but shift pots, skins, tools,
carvings and traps, my library of books,
into the south barn, only our horses
for warmth, nothing and no one to stop me
guiding my life away from damaged ground,
no covered well anywhere in the land
but this. Mum grew pale and died. Candlelit,
Dad sat vigil, then rose up the stone wall
under the timbers my great-grandfathers
used to truss our roof when the valley was
full of trees big enough to fashion masts.

Tenement

Mobile Home

A crick in my left hip as if I need
to walk and walk into night till sun-up
paints the island red. This tin caravan
is full of wind and fire like something wants
out and I guess it is time for that, time
even for murder. Stunning low-back pain
begs the question: *Who, me?* So from the eyes
coiled up in my gut, right after the monk
walks over my grave, erupts the fury,
cold snake, to curve my body to the spin
of the well she's coiled around. From the eyes'
light comes the shoulder wound. *Chrysanthemum.*
From the eyes of those around me comes light.
And in the nest of light rests fledgling light.

Cellar

The bottom dark though starlight above.
And alone and cold so dying takes
ages while people up top come and
go, send down a bucket on a rope,
send down a question, and are always
fine with my answer. In time the world
flips and I'm shucked and start to fall and
don't want to go. The stairs corkscrew. Pink
umbrella opens. Friends are pebbles
in a stream and it's over, done. All
my fast talk. Swallows. The mallard pair
in the daisy field. Bulrushes. Pond.
Willow. I used to talk a lot. Bridge.
The last hot sticky taste of. Yes? Yes?

Tenement

What is behind the door but other doors,
one open, where we see a girl and boy,
dust and slanting sun, startled oak trees, deep
forest, river. Change the lock and we're safe.
Remove windows, stairs, walls. Stars will outgrow
all we love because we set and stars
will always star. They love one another. These
two love each other, the woman and man
fast asleep downstairs between streetcars and
office windows, between sky and pavement,
and we lose them when we look ahead or
back at things outside this world, deep forest,
river. Sleep leaves the impression of words.
Water drips from green moss into a pool.

Basement Suite

Everything looks wet, the barmaid's belly,
the drowned trunks of pool tables, her felt skin
between T-shirt and jeans time and again
blonde, till Uruguay loses, Sweden wins,
and the familiar alley comes sooner
than expected and home too, a grey day
in June, the rest of the family away
rehearsing the end of *The Winter's Tale*.
She eclipsed the screen during set pieces
time and again, the narrow path submerged
past the drowned pool tables to the back door,
out into summer still underwater,
all skies dark and scruffy for an old man,
a football fan at the end of the world.

Hotel Garden

"Hello? Hello? Hello? Are you so far?"
The fishes in the pond when it empties
empty themselves and when it fills again
they fill not as full, not as orange, not
as bright, yet before it empties again
invite others in. They're numerous and
thin as needles. I call but you don't hear.
Again and silence; again, no answer.
Why do we open the door and invite
others to enter when the door's not real?
They won't find what we tell them to find, nor
say in words what they do find. "Hello?
Are you so far?" And in the quiet night
a fish answers water: *Goodbye, goodbye.*

James Bond Above the Palace Gate

Lo, la, this tenebrific decline.
Bojabo! I want to be on top.
Poof. Daylight. The rest. Stop
mithering at every cloud-bitten sign
of trouble. Leap or die –
whoops, damn – before I'm killed off
by their worships' topnots'
hatjinx. What's the chance, by
the by, of falling on your feet when most
of the scheme is littered with slag,
pedestal, platform, dais, throne,
the air clogged with marble dust
and gravity territorial, in love
with itself or a rogue moon at best?

Townhouse
for Dave and Sue

Distilled forest, trees around a clearing
caught inside water's heart that falls and will
fall to great water and find in itself
that which will join and that which will divide;
and strength-to-meet equals need-to-divide,
and light shines from a window set in trees,
a cottage perhaps, a girl at the sill,
but he can't tell her purpose, and she sees
only the drop, a boy at the centre,
and trees falling in the clearing that each
supposes a circle, itself complete,
that includes their new self and body. And
joy in them looks out at the round falling
shared world because it can't do otherwise.

The Ruined Cottage

for Bronwen and Jo

The sorry way she sits the wall is not
at all in line with the large history
of crows who now and then taught carpentry
to settlers, yet I watch her *caw* aloft
in a fresh breeze while my fingers pluck moss,
a small history, aimless and alive,
a fist of green, a fist of stars, a hive,
and so begin, we begin, a clear thought.
To pray for the Old World that died when I
was young and my body bobbed along like
a feather on a stick. To tell stones why
they house and roof nothing but mortal life.
Her wings stutter over the burning land
in a child's attempt to catch the first wind.

IV

Quit This Ground

1.

Winter this year has been too cold
and bright with wind and untold
snow. My knees are chafed red-raw,
my nose drips and my hands are sore,
and all the homestead roofs leak.

Daughter in her coffin is dressed
for a spring wedding, at rest,
they say (I'll see them goddamned),
her last word an O, fingers fanned
like rivers across her breast,
which I hold, chill egg, the last
of the clutch, nipple a beak.

I curried her old horse the night
of the hurricane in spite
of demons, then lay perplexed
all day while flies indulged in sex
in every cranny and nook.

2.

Coffin, bed, lamp and this table
I carted to the stable.
Nearly killed me. Now, on the floor,
I sort my daughter's ribbons
from the pinto's steaming dung,
and curse every board and rung
and nail of this splintered wreck.

Jesus I chant to the bucket,
Christ to the empty bucket,
and lean on the broken door
as contrails pierce the pure world
with feathers as frail as glass.

My daughter's eyes are dull; the song
all her grandmothers' ghosts keen
by the well is true; the leap
over Sharp Mountain is miles deep.
Now the bride-wind blows her word
to God and winter and spring her
lover and frost that won't last.

Picker's Sons

1.

Those we loved are dead
and not as small as when we
buried them, but loud
and everywhere. See? Grandma
in the roofless hall leans on

her cane and asks do
we know what we're at, letting
in all that cold air
and birds, spring rain and dirty
critters? Don't these rough rafters

on night sky describe
the wrecked hull of a ship sunk
deep beyond human
help or hope, lost with all hands?
So I raise my head and look

up past her thin face
at the moon, a herring school,
frozen silver cloud,
mandala that will crack, bust
to fragments. Soon as we shake

hands and start again
life will rain down on us and
death will be precious.
Buddy, we were never seen.
I want you to look at me.

2.

No. I'm shouldered out
across the border of your
country and maybe
gonna pounce on such a dish
as pulled sinew, white bones, crows.

Huddle over down
the treeline house now there is
nothing left but time
to cut firewood, fish the bay.
For me the foghorn is all.

My family's left.
Gone the saltlick calves learn to
want. Your cows cry wolf
but wolves hunt what I know: that
those we love are dead as dirt.

3.

Sure, but remember
they kept us in golden corn,
spuds, rye, alfalfa.
In spring, though their names are gone,
crops still poke up through the weeds.

Remember the town
cousins who drove down to fuck
us in the hayloft
and smoke dope and hypnotize
the city lights till the barn

caught fire? They're still
at it, letting the wind loose
and all the horses
and cows and swallows wheeling
over ash grey nests.

Buddy, they wear coats
in the rain, wait for the word.
Pop from his box shouts
a warning that has in it
nationality, not ours,

but if we listen
we might figure a new barn,
all fresh-cut wood filled
with yellow hay. In *nation*
dwells fire and fire's end.

4.

A barn leaves no trace
once it and a year have burned,
only fireweed.
I orbit the treeline hut
working blind and led by crows,

your full moon running
out to tell me I have run
out of places, used
up wood and wasted what life
you can't shepherd me across.

No more yours and mine.
No borders for owls to blur.
Nothing left but wind,
glints of sun on the freshet,
the night beacon's quick thrust.

Hand

I don't recognize
my own as my own because
an old man's scrawl

as old as the hills
on the fogged-up window
joining sky & field

can't touch birds flying
above the roar of traffic
now the valley's gone

    new winter houses
    delivered by men in trucks
    throw bones at the sky

I take forever
to lace my shoes since fingers
forget all they are

assigned regardless
the birds – the time – infinite
tasks in a ghost wood

it takes forever
to uncloset what I need
for the outer cold

snowlight in the hall
through the open door a claw
poised to crack my skull

I held a brown bird
stunned by a summer window
the name escapes me

The Last House

North

sun on the willow
the woman carries the wash
over the grey dog
asleep by the open door
cliff swallows reclaim the line

years ago we chose
a red butter-soft puppy
who liked us & did
not pee all the long drive home
except when we stopped for gas

I led him gently
to the end of the pasture
& over the fence
to hack through ferns & deadfall
looking for a new way out

I courted island
& city women & once
left him on the boat
where he waited & waited
until everyone had gone

Sky

Elegy Eight
my hands on the steering wheel
her hands in the soil
night numbers flash slim thighs
fingers pull wireworms from spuds

South

I touch alder buds
& fill the bird feeder
transplant iris corms
I've immigrated this deep
sold three houses one condo

cleared a drainage ditch
of clay silt & hurt my back
same year-end I smashed
the glass because she wanted
to fuck the Maritimer

life's done what I said
now I must transform the blood
in my heart and veins
blood of past relationships
sun sinks beneath the swamp

machinery noise
swallows the music that still
means something still yes
to who will say yes heart wide
for the sea wave & tide

but call this heart cave
let current fill rock & still
my cock's as silly
as a penguin with tennis elbow
trying hard to fly

Antarctic Ocean
finish the loose ends won't you
forget the ice cubes
& that big hole in the sky
& all those stars   I will change

East

a crazy man loose
in the valley steals seven
eggs from a hay bale
then beats a girl on the road
threatens to shoot her   all day

blunders windy hills
(we hear him spending ammo)
running deer & descends
by night to steal a rowboat
& goes wild on the next island

the girl visits me
(her face is blue one eye closed)
wearing a gold dress
no one is guilty she says
no one person is to blame

we smoke cigarettes
& hold hands *there's only room*
for one here she says
we look out of the windows
at the strangeness of the world

we drink retsina
her small body fills the place
I watch her all night
carefully no plans no deal
sleep already full of prey

the fox leaps so there's
still time for everything
time's mystery   fox-
glove   red-tailed hawk in the air
mouse in the tall yellow grass

Earth

saw a fox curled stiff
by the London-Brighton tracks
saw a red fox sniff
a cornfield down a roly-
poly Devon hill   saw a fox

leap into highway
traffic south of Vancouver   leap
through metal
the dense median
deep into greener traffic

West

I'm borrowing this
body I need to transform
again the feeling
in the open outhouse wet
dog snug between my knees

how much longer till
my life breaks through this tangle
or my cards max out
October zaps the trees red
maples ruddy the wet dog

tell me what to do
I feel the tenant burning
tell me anything
wisdom takes the green path
ghosts gather round the last house

this plywood hut
that smells of my own brave life
snags all the wide world
in my throat & I can't breathe
maple leaves chase in frenzy

night & debt press
forward pitch me closer to
great difficulty
a grave behind the dug well
easy to lose one's footing

Papa Chaos

Postcards

I don't love you don't
love you the way I used to
wish you were here

I like my penis
how fat & sturdy it feels
ripe bulrush bending

Night

terrible wind yet
under the house the mower drips
oil on a sand tray

so many dark clouds
rolling over our valley
turn every new leaf

first light on alders
dead before it hits the ground
peeps out of rain drops

such cool morning air
the Kiftsgate rose denuded
petals on the step

Hartland Dump

eagles flew through firs
as if the forest owned them
air looked like water

the tollman walked up
the giant hill of garbage
popped a pink umbrella

Dad said *be careful*
my finger went in the road
tar is poisonous

Trap

how full the world is
every night I set a trap
each morning check it

then one hot midnight
as I drift away to sleep
a grey mouse is caught

who belongs to me
the way dreams belong to slaves
& slaves to no one

when I've had my tea
fed the dog & showered we
ride to the bible camp

amid wet green ferns
dark mud & gaping caves
branches cross with light

setting her free
is setting my own heart free
both of us are lost

Pair

in a green barrow
in the little yard we built
the ducks swim circles

cayugas chasing
sunlight & flying water
the last day of spring

now the white duck rests
her head on the drake's blue back
& lets him paddle

BBC World Service

let me hear a thrush
to know it's all right   weeping
birch catches street light

in the dusk windows
shadow boys fight shadow boys
what is this city?

blame & massacre
birds singing from Sri Lanka
the curtains part

a child is caught by
all that spins
all that gnashes

World Trade Centre

and again I pull
my finger from scalding tar
stick it in my mouth

while fierce sun burns him
black   this man my dad   and still
I have high blood pressure

two parts of one thought
fish   eagles   who will cross the field
as if the forest owns us?

who will hold whose hand
once the landfills fill
with land?

Wren

For Stephen G

What the sky interrupts is evidence
of what he can't name
though naming may be evidence of sky.

On earth trees collide, wind pushes inland.
In the ICU
Stephen lies dying or changed. The wren floats

into space, as if life is too much to
live. As if leaves are
birds who fall, and we are best left alone.

Stephen cannot imagine the road west.
It gleams in the last
light through bare cottonwoods, quick slant of rain.

Courtyard

Middle Region

Mountains range the horizon. We commute
the coastal plain north, say no and no to
the radiant haze of burnt gasoline.
Ours. The bus driver rides the brake to shape

his timetable, but we can't recognise
our stops because his time isn't ours.
We close our eyes and follow the snowmelt
downhill, losing a little at each stream,

home at last, too tired to find the key,
so settle for alleys till they are full
of bodies, books sleeping with thin pages,
so frail the slight breeze mixes us up, so

his fury jackals against her sadness
and her nostalgia blooms and thickens
his regret and his nervousness ignites
her strength and the pages shred on chainlink

and we all arrive in the foothills as
bits of snow, bits of mist, and join with smoke
that coils from pits and timber piles serviced
by foreigners trying to burn the earth.

Courtyard

for Denise

A day of dogs when they stop the bombs.
Then leaflets, quiet. Birds outside
the window in the hedge. We know when
it's time to go, to put on frailty

like a disguise until it mimics
the thin branching of time, the burn
of autumn before colours die and
days lie still, the same old door open

each midnight to Mum and Dad fighting,
their fight not ours. Autumn's yellow
was not ours, nor were the blood red leaves,
and starlight fades as the day strengthens,

starlight that lit the river that
led us here and meanders toward
a future distance we measure now,
especially now, in every cell.

Nor was Christmas ours, and not houses
(though gardens were lovely), nor cars,
holidays, countryside, the sea, and
all those times we loved and were loved back,

the moment we made a child out of
almost nothing, what you came with
and I gave away, a child we don't
know yet. We wait by shuttered cafés.

We wait with pigeons (who know to wait
patient as stars who wait for night).
We wait in the warm courtyard and scan
the wild stone hills above the crop line.

Leap

Okay. There's a frog on the moon. The dwarf
hatches when the faulty street light blazes.
Otherwise there's nothing left. The frog leaps
from the moon into space. Into my head.

The old dwarf helps me erect a scaffold
on a beach at dawn. When all's gone and said
the body releases what it wants, or
what it can't hold. The body releases.

The street light blazes. I'm sick of winter.
The long walk home is so feverish that
a brand new language leaps from my head to
the ground. The dwarf smiles, won't lift a finger.

He's been where we were not to go and must
go where we're not to go. The frog leaps from
the ground to the moon, but the dwarf keeps me
company – he knows about the dark and

sudden burning of a sun and how to
have nothing and leave nothing behind. Frog
leaps into space, into my head, onto
the ground. In grace, already committed

to outer night, shame lost, friends lost. In moon-
light the dwarf, joined by others, half human,
helps me erect a scaffold on the beach.
It's dawn, the winter air silver. Every

livid interrupted beauty's easy
to see, yet not to name. My chest hurts. It's
nothing but the start of a cold day, one
hand on the tame head of a piebald beast.

This Perfect

round gold rock in the gut. The smallest spider stops
on its way across the table, red not gold, and
gone when I look again having taken my eyes
off it for the few moments it takes to pencil

a note the doing of which will fix us both in
time to be recovered later by others should
the spider scrawl be copied into a form sweet
and sturdy enough to warrant publication

such publication dependent on a reader
recognizing or being surprised by spider
who has long since quit the table and possibly
abandoned the world altogether and left no

further evidence of existence behind and
another reader to agree though perhaps not
finding the symbol quite as fresh or telling as
the first reader but fair enough okay okay

so long story short the Arachnid Trilogy
sees the light of many printings and the movie
arouses brief interest the sequel bombs and
all that's left is "Who killed the spider?" and kids who

marshal on pillows red spider action figures
who vanish with the light as soon as we begin
to teach the phenomenal mechanical world
which is our business and has nothing to do with

round gold rock in the gut, herald of something small.

Hit Brightness with Brightness

What does my heart know of yours?
If you plan an ambush check the exits.

In a tight spot be polite. Remember
your hidden knife. Keep your distance.

Go to sleep three hours after sunset
and be up an hour before dawn.

Practice until you can shoot a head
of wheat out a bottle in the wind.

The beginning of a fight's a farewell:
if you win you lose. *And if you lose?*

Keep to the middle of the road. Pay
attention to shadows and sunlight.

When you take a prisoner always
stay behind him. Never show fear.

Ask the sword saint to cut pain.
What does your heart know of mine?

Georgia Strait

The boatman says he sees
my life is better now.

I walk home up the hill,
one two three four five crack,

sleep through the day, return
as sun dips low – one sail

white on the water – roll
through Active Pass and slow

slow to Vancouver, slow
through dusk to night that brings

a lean girl to the bus
to arch her long pale neck.

Inked stones. A red sports
car plunges into Blenz

at Broadway and Granville.
Small cappuccino, five

pebbles. Old words call new
words, not copies. Rain on

my leather back. Children
will be born. Far away

I was born, you were born.
One two three four five crack.

Sorcerer

At last I lie down
on my back in the narrow

wooden boat, paddle
the underground river – ink

handprints visible
over the claw marks of cave

bears who once had dens
in these Pyrenees foothills

east of Lourdes – and drift
past a factory chimney,

mother and father
arguing in the shadows,

to a dry stone floor,
sanctuary wall, where rears

the nightmare long hidden
above a herd of bison,

a race of reindeer,
snowy owls out of scale.

Lately, when shaving,
I have noted cervid ears,

the bumps of new horns,
the same staring eyes. Flowers

curl at his feet, sharp
thorns stencil his white forehead.

The Axe of Change

Facilis descensus Averno,
what Sybil said to Aeneas

I say to you, O my pretty
telluric commandos!

I'm swimming on September air,
before the Uzi, before the M-16,

standing in the upstairs
bedroom reading a poem.

Effervescent. A blue floor.
Webby sills. I exercise stability,

long for sunlight, longed
for but ungrasped. You

incomprehensible culture.
Beware the axe of change.

You are too many too fast
to see what's in your way.

Return is tough, the stairs
have caved in, only

the mad would attempt the
attic's shaft of moonlight.

Ancestors

Her refugee family, small
dark men and bosomy women,
invites me aboard their pickup
among the crates and kitchenware
and we gutbucket through the crowds
of carts and barrows to escape.
Not new, this moment, dash of pepper,
hot like her eyes, black sausage,
bread, black bangs jagged across her
white forehead. This time, these killings.

Murder is part of a larger
map I once saw in a shop, yet
she's a chocolate, a surprise
cake, black cat, night.
"I have always been here," she says,
"famous revolutionary
girl waiting for you." We hold hands
in back of the truck. Her finger
is bleeding. "You are mine," she says.

Planes drown the next words.
Her eyes flash *sky, last sun*. Mama
and Grandpapa exchange a glance.
Her dad battles the road, the wheel.

Invention of Flight

Surrey farmland passes the windows,
the original garden slated
for new housing, while commuters nod
in September sunshine and highway
knows it will end at the sea. Hawk sleeps
on a fence post, web salvers glisten
in the stubble, the golf course swallows
the stone-built farm, and I've just woken,
heart high in the gut the way we ride
this bus through it all. Because it yields.

At Ladner Exchange women run dogs
on the old trap circuit. Indian
summer is full of blessings, honest
blessings a hair's-breadth from here. Did I
note the source? A man in a red shirt
is racing toward golden trees, so
I open my pack, unfold blue-lined
foolscap, not sure why this view of fields,
these lines, over and over, while waves
crack pebbles south side of the causeway
and a spooked blue heron plays jaw harp:

When the well is deep the rope is long.
A fierce day at the mountain retreat.
One thing finishes; one thing begins.
Energy under unseen beauty.
Lightness calls up lightness. Frail bucket,
empty; vital fish beyond the earth.

The Stars

for Lorraine

Rain clatters on the roof as we sleep-talk,
phones tucked under each bed, March in both rooms,
the month before April, windows open
to ghostly air. We marry with the new
moon, long known, how we cross the stone beach, climb
the cliff to eagles and raven and chill
wind with pocket pebbles to bury, sticks
to burn, silver rings to bind us, and I
let in your fox brown eyes and see what works
in you that works in me, and know what kills
you killed me too, till the candles stir with
breath as sweet as spring and we perch face to

face on the cliff edge, blue sail on my right,
your left, small boat light in the surf, nothing
less to carry our bodies already
smoke to the sky, ash to the sea, loved ones
west and east, our kingdoms in peril, tribes
burned out of stone forts. It is useless to
choose a direction: current must find us.

At last we swim away from each other
to make the storm less jealous; old stars freeze
the water, earthquakes calve an island, and
another me adores another you
inland.

Utter

Blown an alternator and in tow to Duncan,
past lake and green forests, only a few light clouds
in so-blue sky, a family of four puzzled
by calamity. I called the tow truck. This is
my dad's camper. My son's the son of someone else.

The hottest day of the year we cross the highway
from Canadian Tire and my dog hangs his tongue
all the way to Burger King where the kid's meal includes
a tiny naked girl whose uniform appears
only when she's plunged in ice water. Outside the
library I wait under a tree with Géza
while Lorraine takes Ash inside to find sloops, cannons,
siege machines, and shut my eyes and see down into
the column of my body where water rises –
two three four five six seven – safe looking down, dry
yet, at the swirl in the bole, the cave door below
to let the flood should time announce a change, or light,

don't forget light, though here is dark as dark can be,
summer dark, dark as death, and no sky so far and
no other flourishes, just we who know only
earth and the blackness of earth, tang in our nostrils,
as we wait to see if the water will rise and
drown us or leak away and leave us high and dry,
trapped in our skin and limbs with new problems such as
how to get out, how get down, how get through, and what

to do next. Better watch the eye of the vortex,
fancy word for spin, not get dizzy, and perhaps
then we'll sleep and wake to new events, like Mama
bringing our breakfast or a sunrise to beat all –
eight nine ten. And I do wake to mother and son,
cranky and bored, the library a bust, the dog
hungry, dragonflies everywhere.

VI

Chorale

street lamps light nothing
till one blazes his shadow
on the frozen ground

nothing inside him
but that girl's silk skin & home
he has abandoned

a perfect moment
his breath clouding a pear branch
red buds under ice

      animals gather
      in the clearing we made   sun
      warms them till they sleep

your mother's poodle
staggers in circles   he's old
& will not live long

your mother says sleep
is hard to come by   she left
the house in a dream

the day her husband's
heart quit   *it felt like uphill*
she croons   *don't run rings*

baby don't run rings
the gas fire hisses beneath
your father's blue geese

we walk the path round
the lake   echo the old dog
our lives rough wild things

the monk brings warm clothes
plucks seven straws from a broom
give these to the child

I make a taper
while my son sings explosions
for the winter fire

in heaven we track
satellites circling the world
birds with no season

at dawn deer gather
around us in the clearing
to graze the ashes

black shoes at the door
the ceremony gets hot
I open one eye

woken by a voice
outside my door   the rasp
of coarse sandpaper

stern men hunch over
benches in twilight finishing
things I once began

red shining dust hangs
hotter than eucalyptus
in the roof shadow

the wood cedar from
the smell of it   we do think
we meet who we want

to meet when it's time
& always at night   near dawn
in spring   before birds

my forty-seventh
birthday Dad breaks into song
...the dark sacred night

I run my bike out
at dawn   stumble on timbers
the well-house gave up

my dog & I rush
the salt fog & the mountain
for one glimpse of sea

a spire of white smoke
from the clearing where the monk
is building a shrine

Géza (5/2/1994 – 12/18/2005)

Every living thing will die, but I was
not ready, though you told me with
your eyes and body on that last long walk
through the dark when you realized the distance,
Vancouver to Steveston, and stood still, full
of invisible words, and spoke, then put
your head down, trotted by my side over
the bridge, past cars and cars till December sun
rose and lit blueberry fields for us
in Richmond, alders yellow in the distance
above a red twig sea. I loved you
then as I loved the world, for you
were in the world and I was by your side,
and all else was to come or in the past.

The emperor of the South Sea was called Shu (Brief), the emperor of the North Sea was called Hu (Sudden), and the emperor of the central region was called Huntun (Chaos). Shu and Hu from time to time came together for a meeting in the territory of Huntun, and Huntun treated them very generously. Shu and Hu discussed how they could repay his kindness. "All men," they said, "have seven openings so they can see, hear, eat, and breathe. But Huntun alone doesn't have any. Let's try boring him some!" Every day they bored another hole, and on the seventh day, Huntun died.

– Zhuangzi (in Watson, 1964)

Acknowledgements

Thanks to the Canada Council for support during the writing of this book, to Patricia Young for her invaluable friendship and support, and especially to my editor Jan Zwicky for hearing and helping to shape the whole manuscript.

The following poems, some in earlier versions, have already appeared in print. A bow to the editors. "Feast" in *Long Journey: Contemporary Northwest Poets* (David Biespiel, editor); "The Last House" in *Fiddlehead*; "Ancestors" in *Poetry Northwest*; "The Stars" in *Grain*; "Subdivision," "Manchester," and "Dumpster" in *Event*; "Hand" in *The Literary Review of Canada*; "Basement Suite," "Cellar," "Lost Countryside," and "When Hawks Stop Hunting" in *The Malahat Review*; "Courtyard" in *Rocksalt: An Anthology of Contemporary B.C. Poetry* (Mona Fertig and Harold Rhenisch, editors); "Broken Roof" in *Dream Catcher*.

Michael Kenyon was born in Sale, England and has lived on the West Coast since 1967. His work has been shortlisted for the Commonwealth Writers' Prize, the SmithBooks/*Books in Canada* First Novel Award, the Baxter Hathaway Prize in fiction, *The Malahat Review* Novella Prize, *PRISM international*'s fiction contest, the Journey Prize, and the National and Western Magazine Awards. He divides his week between Pender Island and Vancouver, having in both places a private therapeutic practice.